What Christians Should Know About...

Their Value to God

Steve and Chris Hepden

Sovereign World

ISBN: 1 85240 239 3

SOVEREIGN WORLD LIMITED
P.O. Box 777, Tonbridge, Kent TN11 0ZS, England.

Typeset and printed in the UK by Sussex Litho Ltd, Chichester, West Sussex.

Contents

1

Are you Lost?

Pigs!

Working with pigs may have its benefits, but it certainly has its down side. The smell gets to you. It not only gets to you, it gets into you! It is not something that fades away as you leave in the evening to go home. It gets into your clothes and worse – it gets into your skin. You carry it, almost as part of you, and people know!

The story of the son who worked with pigs in Luke 15:11-32, and the way his father responded, introduces us very clearly to the way in which God as a Father values us.

Family feud? Never!

From the beginning it seems to be a tragic story because it takes a major crisis for one of the children to ask for their inheritance before the death of their father. The younger son was getting out, he had had enough. Maybe he had his reasons, he was probably right to do it but he was acting in a rebellious way and, under the law, the penalty for his rebellion was death by stoning (see Deuteronomy 21:18-21). He had decided to go and was not coming back.

There would have been great embarrassment for the family in the village and beyond. For the son to ask for his inheritance before the father had died was like saying, 'I wish you were dead!' It is possible that legally he did have a right to ask but it would have humiliated his father. It seems as though he didn't care. He took all that was due to him and disappeared, as far away as possible.

Our pain

Maybe you can identify with him. Family feuds and crises can lead to so much pain and destruction. There can be much hatred and bitterness and so many feel rejected because of these family issues. The rejection that results undermines basic family values such as affection, love and acceptance. It erodes worth and value. You can feel like giving up on life, because when your family seem against you, and misunderstand you, you wonder what the point of life **is**.

So, the younger son wasn't coming back. He got together all that he had, including his pain, and left. There was something inside driving him. It seemed as though he had lost his identity, so he was going to do all he could to find himself. He also had a lot of money and until the money ran out, he had a lot of friends.

Can you understand his predicament? He has to get away, deny everything, blame everyone else and get the anger and the pain out of his system.

Even though you feel the same pain, you may never go as far as this son, so you learn to internalise it. You feel useless and hopeless. When people ask you how you are, you tell them what you think they want to hear, not how you really feel.

Money can't buy me...
The story shows us that the son squandered all of his wealth on wild living. He was looking for something beyond his money. While he had money he had friends, but when the money ran out, so did the friends!

Isn't life like that? People give you value and esteem because you have something they want. It does you good in the short term. Money buys love for a while, yet it is never the love we long for. There is no lasting value in that kind of love.

People will say and do things to get what they want and it's easy to be deceived by this. They say the right things, the things we want to hear – particularly about ourselves. But it is so superficial because when the difficult times come and we look around for help and support, no one is there. Where are the friends who said all those nice things about me? Gone like smoke dispersing in the wind.

Surely things can't get worse?
The son had such a wonderful time living wildly. The parties! The

relationships! The headaches! But still, that feeling of emptiness and loneliness. The story talks about a famine coming after he had spent all his money. Things went from bad to worse – from worse to even worse than worse!! He had nothing. His friends had disappeared long ago. He had no one, no food, no life, and no value. He had to do something.

From riches to rags!
This young man was from a good and probably wealthy family, yet look at him now. Working with pigs. What did he really think of himself? It could have been a time when a sense of failure and defeat made him feel a useless fool, hopeless and worthless, maybe even suicidal because 'no-one cared'.

And don't forget the smell! It got into everything he had as well as his skin. It was as if he had been marked, and when he ventured out people crossed to the other side of the road to avoid him. What a transformation! The son who had everything now had absolutely nothing!

All the lonely people
A song that was written many years ago but that still has great significance to today's society encapsulates the mood of this story.

> *'All the lonely people where do they all come from?*
> *All the lonely people where do they all belong?'*
> (Eleanor Rigby, Lennon/McCartney,
> Parlophone Records, 1966)

It is possible to be surrounded by people, or even be in church, and yet feel so alone. Where do **you** belong? The son had a decision to make. The power to choose was his and it is also **yours**.

An honest appraisal
It's amazing how low we get before we start coming to our senses. The idea of being a slave back at home was a thousand times better than this! This son thought clearly and then took

some action. Even in the midst of his own pain, and the memories of what had happened at home, he knew what he had to do.

He took responsibility!
In all life's difficulties it is easier to blame someone else and adopt the role of a 'poor victim'. There was probably an injustice in the family in this story, yet the son saw the part he had played and wanted to put it right. He left home in rebellion, no doubt with harsh words spoken. He knew deep in his heart that he had to put things right.

He went back
He had nothing, he felt nothing, and he was nothing! Words like 'self-esteem', 'self-worth', and 'self-acceptance' meant nothing to him. He was finished. He had no sense of value. A slave's life was the only thing he thought was available to him.

Yet it was at his lowest point that he sensed a flicker of hope deep within: 'Maybe I can go back and put things right? I've nothing to lose because I've already lost it all.'

This was his attitude as he started his long journey home. It is amazing how strong and resilient the human spirit is when everything else has gone. Something deep within stirred to draw him back to his father.

Even in the depth of despair and deprivation he found a strength to make some right choices. So can we because we have that same response in our spirits. The only thing we can do is return!

The Father's love
Little did he know that his father had been so concerned for him that it affected not only his work but also his life. Day after day, instead of working the farm, he had spent the time in the field by the road looking into the distance, just to see if perhaps his son might return. There was a deep longing for his son. A love that could not be extinguished no matter what had happened.

Amazingly enough this father was not angry, vengeful, or plotting how to deal with the son, but was longing to have him back. His love for his son had not diminished. It had stayed constant!

The son didn't know this and was preparing a speech for his father and as he got nearer to home, he wondered what consequences would face him.

He was in for a surprise, because instead of rebuking him, the father loved him all the more. As he saw his father running down the road towards him he rehearsed his speech with some panic. Instead of the father throwing stones at him, he threw his arms around him and kissed him. I think I would have kept my distance until he had at least showered! Yet he was so overwhelmed at seeing his son, so overflowing in his love, that the sight and smell only seemed to increase his compassion. You see, in that culture, a man of stature would never run in public, but walk in a slow, stately and dignified manner. The father however, was so filled with love and compassion and had such an urgency to be with his son again, that he ignored the fact that it might offend somebody.

Value

Probably you, like me, would feel that the father had some issues with his son that needed dealing with. Maybe later they would talk, but what was in the father's heart was not bitterness and anger, but a love that seems rare these days and a sense of acceptance that seems impossible.

'He still cares,' thought the son. 'He does love me. He still thinks well of me.' That strengthened him deep within because he felt valued and certainly loved.

After the hugs and kisses the father told his servants to bring a robe. Not any old thing to cover his ragged, stinking appearance, but the best robe – a costly and beautifully embroidered one – one that felt too heavy to wear. It did more than cover his tatty clothes, it touched his heart. 'He really does care for me,' thought the son.

Then the father put a ring on his son's finger. Sons wore rings as a sign and seal of their sonship. His original ring had gone to the pawnshop long ago and the father didn't even ask where it was! His feet were bare, and only slaves were barefoot. He was happy to remain a slave, but the father had different ideas. Out came the shoes and the son felt so good because he was accepted! He had felt so devalued, but the person whom he felt would make things worse in fact made them better!

A party?

What else could happen? Out came the fatted calf to feast on in celebration. Not a scrawny old chicken here, but the best. Good old dad! His son is back and who cares about the expense? The son who was lost is found. It's a time for rejoicing. Some of us may feel that this is too good to be true, because we hold another perception of fathers.

Punishment

The father may have said, 'How could you do this to me after all I've done for you?' Then the guilt and shame would have come and we would have been back to the start of things again. There would probably have been a sharp rebuke or maybe something more violent than that. You may begin to feel as though the goalposts are being moved all the time and you can never keep up – the fear of punishment just becomes greater.

Passivity

With others it may seem as if the father doesn't really care. He really can't be bothered and as usual you feel ignored, let down and rejected. He has better things to do than to consider you!

Perfectionism

'This time you will do it my way; you will do it my way because I am right and you are wrong and you will obey me in every specific detail!' Have you ever heard that? Has someone tried to tell you that you are useless and have no right to an opinion about anything?

Performance

Performance is the 'you must always work harder to please me' pressure and 'you had better do it right or you will do it again!' You will then strive without rest, because you can never do enough to pay him back.

Power

All of this adds up to being under the control of another who tries to impose his will on us. Can you see that **this father** did **not** have any of these characteristics? He showed a love that actually drew the son back to himself. This is exactly what our Father God wants to do with us.

The Father's Heart

Right at the beginning of things, you see something that is quite amazing about the response of the father. It seems as though the son had to go away in order to come back, and the father didn't complain by word or deed but gave him the inheritance that would have been his. Doesn't it usually come after death? What would you have done? At least get angry and certainly not give him a penny! Yet this father gave, and gave, and gave again. Even when the son returned with nothing, the father gave again. Doesn't that say something about his character and personality? What a sense of value he placed in his son! Such unconditional love; no strings attached, no repaying the debt. No performance for affection, no doing or saying anything to gain the father's pleasure. All of this devalues worth, esteem and a sense of value, yet his father did nothing but accept him as he was because his love for his son was so much greater than all of these things.

Doesn't it remind you of another Father? God as a Father is all of this and more. This is such a perfect picture of His love for us. He accepts us as we are and wants to give us His love unconditionally, without cost or any need for us to prove anything.

This father knew that a son is a son, is a son, and that's that! Surely it's the same for us. Whatever happens, we are sons (male and female) and God as our Father knows that. We need to know it as well. The father knew that his son could never not be his son. Finally the son also realised that this was his father's heart.

There's more!

The depth of the love of Father God for us is much greater. Remember that we are not just sons but we live in Him as well. We are attached to the family we are born into. We are born, and there is relationship. In the same way our relationship with God starts with us **being in** Christ. We start **being in** and we continue **being in**.

This is the extent of the value we have in Him. Nothing can compare with this. It is beyond anything that this world could offer. Surely this is the security we desire and long for. Remember we can do nothing to gain this. It is only by His grace and He values us more than we realise.

2

Me Valuable?

'What does God see in me?'
'How can God value me?'
'Who am I that God could ever love me?'
'God is too big to care about me!'

These are just a few of the comments made by people who have a problem with how they think God sees them. It's a problem that brings insecurity and condemnation and this can make it difficult to respond in worship to God. It feels as if something has to be done to get on His side again, to please Him and to be accepted by Him.

When these statements about yourself seem impossible to answer, the only way to cope is to push the thoughts down somewhere within, deny they are there, and get on with life until the next time.

Denial doesn't provide the inner peace that you hope for! You may think that if you try to please God by doing something for Him then everything will be all right, because the pressure will go and God will be satisfied with you, at least for the time being.

Many of us find it very difficult to imagine that anyone could ever think good things about us, and God even less! Sometimes we react negatively when we hear someone say something nice about us, particularly if we have not been used to it. If we struggle with people saying good things about us, how much more will we struggle when we hear that God accepts us and loves us?

Isn't it true that this is the sort of response being given consistently by many Christians, who we think are OK! Maybe you are one of them? There are so many of us who always question God's love for us. If we say, 'Does He really love me?'

are we in fact saying 'Does He really care?' This in itself will undermine much in our faith and could ultimately spiritually cripple us. If we believe that God doesn't love or care for us, what do we do, where do we go?

By making these statements we actually devalue God's judgement of us, because if He says He loves and accepts us, and we have problems receiving that love and acceptance, then we will always have difficulty in valuing ourselves properly. Let's ask ourselves who is right – God or us? Of course we say 'God!' – until the next time! And so the conflict goes on and on. The problem is that we never bury our problems dead, they always come back to haunt us. What goes around comes around!

Value, esteem, acceptance, worth, image,
'I'm OK, you're OK!'
Everywhere we look, advertisements, magazines or one of the many self-help books are telling us how to be different, to change who we are. They tell you that you can change your image by using some cosmetics, or even change your physical features by having surgery. The effect of all of this is to create a feeling within us that insists, 'I need to look better. I need to look like him or her to be accepted.' When we try this approach and are disappointed, our sense of worth, esteem and value plummets. If we are not basically happy with who we are, it is just another short step to thinking that other people are probably unhappy with us as well. Finally we reach the conclusion that God feels the same way too!

What do you believe about yourself?
● Do you believe that there is something wrong about you?
● Do you believe that your self-esteem and worth is defined by the approval or disapproval that you receive from others?
● Do you believe that you have to please everyone to gain acceptance and approval?
● Do you believe that your worth depends on the sort of education you've had?
● Do you have to be right about everything to feel good?
● Do you believe that if you look good it will affect you sense

13

of personal value?

- Do you believe that if you had more money everything would be all right about yourself?

These questions may highlight the way you see yourself and will consequently put pressure on you to do something about how you feel. Instead of striving again to be different, why don't you wait and understand a few more things before making choices that will only lead to more pain.

There is something within most of us that will all too easily criticise and condemn us. Because we do not measure up to the standards we think we should, we somehow allow ourselves to be shaped by the influences of the world and those given us by our parents and other people we look up to.

It is true to say, that one of the biggest issues in the Christian church today revolves around the way we see ourselves. It affects the way we are, the way we live our lives, the way we behave, the way we show our emotions and feelings. If we continually feel worthless and useless, our emotions, our feelings and our behaviour will reflect that and will ultimately affect the way we see God and the way we think God sees us.

The mental confusion and emotional conflict of a distorted self-image produces a downward spiral of negativity. You feel trapped in a form of religion and forced to make an effort to do something to get out. All that really happens, even if you try to get out, is that you become aware of your own inability to do so. This pushes you further down the spiral and the feeling of failure grows. Ultimately your relationship with God is undermined because you think there is no way out.

Do you see the power of the way we think? It just takes a tiny seed to be sown in the mind and before long all sorts of negativity begins to bear fruit. The problem is that such seeds take root strongly and they continually erode our self-esteem and value. Perhaps we should look at Psalm 91 again!

So what are we to do? How can we change? This is where we need to take a quantum leap in the way we see ourselves. God has a lot to say about the way **He** sees and thinks about us. Our problem is how do **we** encompass the change, and deal with the pain, involved in our beginning to see things **His** way?

It starts with us, because God has always been constant in the way He has valued us. Our response must be to let Him communicate this to us and to allow ourselves to accept it. We have a definite part to play and it is important for us to see that. There has to be a choice made – a decision of the will.

Emotions may be powerful but the will is a force of nuclear proportions! God will not cross it unless you give Him permission to. The enemy will try to, but you have the power to stop him. Therefore wilfully opening yourself to God is vital. This is the risk you need to take. Are you ready? It will mean giving control over to Him. Yes, that's right, 'letting go.' This is the key; this is the risk. So make a choice – open yourself up to the Father's love.

We saw in chapter one that the Father accepts and values us even though we might think we are failures, or have done something so bad that we think God would never accept us. We saw that the younger son eventually took responsibility for his actions and the father was already waiting for him, to receive him back as a son.

Security in the Father's love is fundamental to our faith and lifestyle and it gives us the right foundation to live and cope day by day. We will want to tell others about the God who accepts and loves us and how we are secure in that love no matter what comes our way.

Before going on to look at things in a more personal way, we need to consider some basic biblical and foundational issues about how God regards us and what He thinks about us.

God's Covenant

As children of God, we need to understand how He views us in relation to the covenant He has made with us. Our personal value, worth and self-esteem all stem out of this covenantal relationship.

A covenant is basically an agreement. God's covenant was established with His people thousands of years ago when He basically said, 'If you obey my commandments and follow me, I will bless you.' Much of it was summed up in keeping the law with its rules and regulations and entering into a form of sacrifice, which satisfied God through the shedding of animal's blood.

There was a wonderful response from God to His people, *'Now if you obey me fully and keep my covenant, then out of all the nations you will be my treasured possession. Although the whole earth is mine, you will be for me a kingdom of priests and a holy nation'* (Exodus 19:5-6). The heart of God was for His people.

This agreement went so far, but something else was necessary to bring the people into a relationship with their God. That something else was **someone else**: Jesus, the Son of God! He was recognised as the 'Lamb of God' and every previous sacrifice from the old covenant became fulfilled in Him as He was given up 'unto death' as a Lamb. This sacrifice formed the beginning of a new covenant. This covenant was still about the shedding of blood, but this time it was God Himself who was personally involved.

This shows us how much God loves and values and accepts us. It is to the point of death and is the focus of the Gospel. John 3:16 sums it up so very clearly, *'God so loved the world that he gave his one and only Son that whoever believes in him should not perish but have eternal life.'* This initiative is not ours, but comes so personally from God. It is vitally important to see this, because it puts the gospel into its true perspective.

It is amazing that the same response from God in Exodus now comes to us in the new covenant. The apostle Peter explains it clearly in 1 Peter 2:9-10, *'But you are a chosen people, a royal priesthood, a holy nation, a people belonging to God, that you may declare the praises of him who called you out of darkness into his wonderful light. Once you were not a people, but now you are the people of God; once you had not received mercy, but now you have received mercy.'* Do you see the significance of this? Not only are we accepted, but treasured as well!

The Blood and the Cross

God makes it clear in His word that He has only one answer to every need we have. This is found in His Son, Jesus Christ. Jesus has become a substitute for us in life and in death. He died instead of us for our forgiveness and lives instead of us so that we can overcome, day by day, in the power of the Holy Spirit. The cross deals with what we are and the blood deals with what we have

16

done. It is a complete sacrifice and we can, by faith, enter in and know the benefits, which in turn will confirm our standing before God and consequently, our value before Him.

As we begin to understand the value that God places upon the blood of His Son, we will know its value for us. Throughout the old covenant God was satisfied when He saw the blood of animals shed. *'When I see the blood, I will pass over you'* (Exodus 12:13). The value of the blood was such that it turned away the judgements of God. This culminated in the shedding of the blood of Jesus and that wholly satisfied God. It happened at the cross and it happens now! *'We have not been redeemed by silver and gold but with the precious blood of Jesus, a lamb without blemish or defect'* (1 Peter 1:18-19). If God can accept the payment of the blood of His Son for our sins as the price for redemption, then it can be acceptable for us! We can do nothing to gain that acceptance except have faith in the power of the shed blood of Jesus.

Not only does the blood satisfy God, it also gives us a way in which we can stand clean before Him. There is no barrier, and if there was, nothing we could do would remove it. The operation of the precious blood has removed that barrier and I can approach God with confidence because of the finished work of Jesus. If I try in my own strength to do something that would make God accept me, I fail. So, I do nothing except seek the presence of God by the way of the shed blood. I approach God on His merit alone and never on the basis of my attainment.

Someone has said that the Cross means when God saw us at our worst, He loved us the most!

The scripture is clear about God's response to us, *'If God is for us who can be against us?'* (Romans 8:31). We cannot answer the 'Accuser' with our good conduct – it doesn't work. We answer with and by the effectiveness of the blood of Jesus and the enemy has no grounds for attack. All that attempting to please Him by trying to be humble or loving does, is show us that there is an inability to get it right. We cannot succeed on our own and in our own strength. The covenant of God shows us that He has done it on our behalf and that nothing we can do will match that. Therefore our value comes from Him, through Him and in Him.

3

Who do you Think
you Are?

How do you see yourself?
If you had the opportunity to describe what kind of person you
think you are, what would you say? It seems that most people
would, on the whole, respond in a negative fashion and be critical
of themselves. We all have opinions of ourselves, and most of
them are not good, particularly if we are under pressure with the
problems of life. We are constantly bombarded by voices telling
us we need to be better. Maybe we have listened to too many
adverts saying, 'buy this and feel good,' or maybe our school
teachers used to tell us, 'it's not good enough.' Perhaps our
parents tried to make us do better and be better. All the time there
was that nagging feeling that if only we could respond to all these
demands, we would gain a little more self-esteem and value –
enough to get us through the day or a difficult period. Of course
we never can reach these targets and we find ourselves slipping
further away, believing that nothing will ever change because we
cannot change ourselves!

As we interact with people day by day, it is easy to create for
ourselves a wrong picture of what we are really like. If we feel
inferior or insecure in a friend's presence, we may try either to be
like them or react against them in some way. We tend to dislike
who we are and want to change to be like them, or someone else!

The image we have of ourselves is formed mostly through
interpersonal relationships. Our self-image is the result of our
interpretation of involvement and communication with others. It
is the result of what we think others are saying about us. In fact it
is generally **not** what they are **actually** saying or thinking. We
presume more than we know. We take it on board and it becomes
a self-deception.

Our self-image is formed during early childhood with concepts, attitudes and memories of interaction with parental figures – good and bad. We have an ability to deal with our experiences by suppressing or repressing them, but if we don't face up to the pain of our past, things will just become worse. Children all too often respond clearly to the experience but do not seem to have the ability or capacity to interpret the experience positively and that can have repercussions in later life as emotional pain is denied. Some memories will be pleasant, others traumatic, but whether good or bad they help form our self-image.

Because our judgement of ourselves begins during childhood, patterns of thought are established that become 'our way of seeing things', our world view, and this affects us in later years, often deeply, and influences our responses as adults. If you have been told for years that you are 'no-good' or 'useless', this lie, because that is what it is, will embed itself into your mind and affect you in adulthood as you firstly believe it and then act accordingly. It is easy to believe that you can never change, that you will always be the same, because at the end of the day it's your fault anyway! So a perception, the way you see things, or yourself, becomes firmly established. Your perception of yourself may not be the truth from God's perspective!

It is easy too, not to trust yourself, to become overtly preoccupied with your problems and then not correctly perceive what others feel about you and the situation you are in. You mistakenly believe that other people feel the same about you as you do! This becomes a vicious cycle and you cannot be who you would like to be because of the fear of rejection, and it is better to withdraw even though this is painful.

What you think of yourself will clearly influence the kind of life you live, the way you behave and the way you respond and react. Also if you see **yourself** in a wrong way, it is likely that you will see **others** in a wrong way!

Self-analysis test
Look at the comments below, consider how many of them relate to you, and mark yourself honestly according to the way you see yourself. The maximum you can score is 5 points per statement if

you **agree** strongly with them, and zero if you look at the statements and **disagree** strongly with them. Potentially, you could score a maximum of 75 points and a minimum of zero. This will give you an indication of the level of self-esteem, worth and value that you have. It may be that someone has said these things to you and that you have believed them over the years. Mark yourself accordingly.

1. I'm stupid
2. I'm not worth anything
3. I'm no good
4. I feel inferior
5. I'll never be able to do it
6. I'm useless
7. I don't like the way I look
8. I'm a failure
9. There must be something wrong with me
10. No one loves me
11. I'm lonely
12. I want to be like him or her
13. No one must ever know what I am feeling
14. I'm not supposed to cry; they don't like it
15. There I go again!

The higher the score, the higher the possibility of you falling into the categories below:

● You don't like yourself!
● You can't believe people would like you.
● You don't understand how God can love you.
● You don't know what to do to change all of this.

The struggle for self-acceptance
The pressure on us to do something to be accepted, to conform, to achieve, to be better, or to make a favourable impression has never been so great. But the more we try, the harder it gets and the heavier we fall. Comments like 'I must do well... I must not fail... I must succeed', often push us into the unreality where we become a victim of our own needs and end up disliking ourselves even more as our esteem and sense of value decline. The best

thing to do is to smile, push the pain down, be happy, be Christian and forget the personal problems. Or on the other hand, be aggressive, manipulative, controlling or all three whenever you choose, so that you can bury the problem in a different way in order to focus on how you can get others to give you all that you desire. The trouble is that you just bury the problem alive and put off the issue until another day. But 'another day' is never in your control and it just may creep up on you unexpectedly.

What kind of person would you like to be?
A confident person with a good self-image, a good sense of value and worth accepted by others and able to cope daily? Of course, but is it really possible? Look at the following 6 points with an open heart because **it is possible** for you to attain **all** of them. However you feel, whatever you think about yourselves, whatever has happened in the past, whatever you have done to yourself or others, it is still possible for you to be this kind of person.

1. To love yourself
You're part of God's creation 'fearfully and wonderfully made'.

2. To understand yourself
Being aware of your strengths and weaknesses, you are able to grow towards maturity.

3. To know what you want
You have and can express confidence in moving forward.

4. To know where you are going
Vision is a word you understand and you are not afraid to set new goals and still live in reality.

5. To think positively
You are not interested in denial. You do not transfer blame or become overwhelmed by problems.

6. To behave appropriately
Your reactions and behaviour are revealed in how you handle each

situation with skill!

Following on from that, you will now be able to get to the place where people in your company feel:

- **Secure** because they know where they stand with you. They are not intimated by you or feel that you are afraid of them.

- **Trusted** because they know you won't judge, criticise or abuse them.

- **Confident** because you will encourage them and facilitate them.

- **Understood** by you and not patronised.

- Not **undermined** and **deceived**, because you are not perfect and will acknowledge your own weaknesses, and will take responsibility for your actions as and when necessary.

Your first response might be, 'Help! How can I ever get there? It's outside my ability. I can never do it.' But you **can do it**, and we want to help by showing you how! Can you believe it? If **He** says it, **yes!**

4

What does God Really Think About me?

If we can really find out what God thinks and says about us it will give us a greater assurance and security to look at our own lives in a positive manner and live day by day with a good sense of value and esteem.

We are made with certain inherent needs in life. We have a desire to be satisfied with who we are and what we can receive as we walk through life.

It can be summed up in three parts:
● A sense of belonging
● A sense of worth
● An ability to cope

A sense of belonging
This is the need to be wanted and to know and feel that you are wanted. To know that you are accepted and also enjoyed by others, giving a sense of security. There is nothing so good as others wanting to be in your company because they enjoy your presence.

A sense of worth
This is about value and self-esteem. I know that I'm OK, I am appreciated, I have something to offer, I am worth something. This is an awareness that we are unconditionally loved, which means that we are accepted for who we are not for what we do!

An ability to cope
This is the confidence that we have to get through the day – an ability to cope and meet life's challenges. We know that we can do it! Even when stressful situations arise, we know that we can

get through. It is an awareness of peace and rest at the end of the day because we have made it!

One of the key areas of power in the life of Jesus was the way He saw himself. It was summed up in a very positive self-acceptance with strong self-esteem and value, and manifested itself in a sense of total security as He faced the difficult issues of life. It became the foundation that allowed Jesus to leave the carpenter's workshop and go out and proclaim the good news of the kingdom of God.

Jesus was able to fulfil His Father's call because of His relationship with His Father, so clearly emphasised and underlined at His baptism. It was there that the expression of His Father's love released Him to begin His ministry.

Luke 3:21-22 sums it up in about 4 sentences. Around 50 short words, yet such a foundational key to propel Jesus onward to His task. It was a crucial time because it was this incident with His Father, who interrupted the baptism of Jesus with an incredible response of lavish affection, that gave Him the impetus He needed to move on in the will of the Father. It is also important for us because it is the same love of the Father that has been given to us!

As Jesus came out of the Jordan at His baptism, and for a few seconds stood praying, heaven actually opened and two things seemingly simultaneously happened. The Holy Spirit descended on Him and clothed Him with a power and authority, and a voice spoke out of the open heaven. It was the voice of the Father.

I wonder what the people who were there heard? I know what Jesus heard, and this was enough for him to embark on over 3 years of ministry.

As the Holy Spirit empowered Him, the Father expressed the deep emotional cry of a very personal response to His son. It was as though the whole world needed to hear the Father's cry as well as His Son. It was a declaration and the sealing of family relationship at its greatest!

'You are my son...' This is belonging! Jesus belonged to the Father.

'Whom I love...' This is worth! Jesus was highly valued and esteemed by the Father.

'With you I am well pleased.' This is an ability to cope. Jesus could rest in the trust and pleasure of the Father day by day.

In this place there is no pressure to perform or the need to work in order to be accepted. Jesus had to do nothing to please the Father, but just rest in His love. He had nothing to prove! The Father was saying, 'You are my son, chosen and marked by my love, you are the focus of my delight and the pride of my life.'

Jesus needed nothing else. He had received confirmation of who He was, He received unconditional love and acceptance, which was not based on a pressure to be, to conform, to perform, or to please. The Father was pleased because of who Jesus was, not what He was going to do. No wonder Jesus felt safe as He went out into the towns and villages of Israel. He knew who He was and was secure enough in Himself and His Father's love to go and fulfil His calling.

Everyone needs to know that they are loved and approved of. Where was our first recognised source? Surely it was our family, and it was the same when the Father and the Holy Spirit affirmed Jesus, the Son. He was able to go out with His Father's commission and a great sense of esteem and value. His worth was in no way determined by what others thought of Him, but only in His Father's love. His performance was not driven by the pressure of having to please, because He started with the Father's pleasure. There was nothing else to do and nothing to prove!

As Jesus went about His task with His disciples, it became so clear that here was someone who was different. It wasn't so much the miracles, although they were important, but more noticeably the confident lifestyle and secure attitude. He knew who He was to the point of saying so!

This principle is so important for us to grasp. We need to shift away from thinking about how **we** see and value ourselves. God sees us in the same way as He saw Jesus! He expresses it to us just as He did to His son at the River Jordan.

We are His sons! We are adopted into His family and accepted totally by Him. We belong to the Father, just like Jesus!

We are loved! This is unconditional love. We are highly valued and esteemed by the Father, just like Jesus!

He is pleased with us! We can have a confidence to cope and get through the day. We can rest in the trust and pleasure of the

Father day by day, just like Jesus! He delights in us!

When God made man and woman on the sixth day, He saw that everything was very good and then rested on the seventh day. Therefore the man and woman started their lives in God's **rest** and in the knowledge that they were part of God's **very good** creation!

Throughout the Bible there are many references to the fact that God highly values us as His creation. He is for us and longs to be with us.

● Genesis 1:31 states, *'And God saw every thing that he had made, and behold, it was very good.'*

God sees the works of His hands being more than simply 'good', they are **very good**. God saw us that way at the very beginning and He hasn't changed His mind!

● Ephesians 1:6 says, *"To the praise of the glory of his grace, wherein He has made us accepted in the beloved.'*

The 'beloved' is the Lord Jesus Christ, the well-beloved Son of God – the Son of His love. He has chosen us in Him, and it is through Him that these mercies have been conferred on us.

● Zephaniah 3:17: *'The LORD thy God in the midst of thee is mighty; he will save, he will rejoice over thee with joy; he will rest in his love, he will joy over thee with singing.'*

The fact that God rejoices over us is fantastic. Who are we to receive that? It is grace and we can do nothing to change His love to us!

● Ephesians 1:3-5: *'How we praise God, the Father of our Lord Jesus Christ, who has blessed us with every blessing in heaven because we belong to Christ. Long ago, even before he made the world, God chose us to be his very own through what Christ would do for us; He decided then to make us holy in his eyes, without a single fault – we who stand before him covered with his love. His unchanging plan has always been to adopt us into his own family by sending Jesus Christ to die for us. And he did this because he wanted to!'*

This shows that our God is not a tyrant full of doom and gloom but a God who has chosen to accept us and bless us. Not because He **had** to, but because He **wanted** to.

- I John 3:1: *'See how very much our heavenly Father loves us, for he allows us to be called his children – think of it – and we really are!'* But since most people don't know God, naturally they don't understand that we are His children. We are under the favour of God and He has lavished upon us a quantity and quality of love that is beyond us!

- Ephesians 2:10: *'For we are God's workmanship, created in Christ Jesus to do good works, which God prepared in advance for us to do.'* We are His handiwork – works of art loved and valued by Him.

Our self-esteem then, comes from Him and Him alone and there is **nothing** that we can do to gain this, there is nothing we can do to earn this and it is not based on anyone else or their opinion!

The enemy attacked Jesus in the wilderness with three temptations in the key areas we have looked at. The enemy wanted Jesus to prove **Himself**, to prove His **identity** and to prove His **calling**. But Jesus had no need to prove anything. God had given Him identity, value and security and that was enough!

As we consider our own trials, temptations and the tribulations of establishing our own identity in God, we can use the words that the Father said to His Son, because they are the same words that the Father is saying to us! In the midst of accusations and condemnation from the enemy regarding our identity, we can do what Jesus did and speak out these 'Words of God' and live in victory day by day. Just as Jesus had nothing to prove, neither have we!

5

I Am!

If there were one word that could summarise the Christian Faith, it would probably be 'relationship.' It is worked out in a relationship with God that is vertical, and relationships with others that are horizontal. Our faith then, is founded and built on relationships.

Relationships govern the way in which we see God through Jesus, the way we see each other, and of course, the way in which we see ourselves. 'Relationship' is the place where acceptance, esteem and value begin to grow and strengthen our inner lives.

Jesus didn't just want His disciples to **understand** Him, or to know **about** Him, but to **know Him!** We need God, but we also need each other, because it is this that will bring an understanding and acceptance of who we are.

Today's society is full of conflict in relationship. We cry out for relationship but then find it all too easy to walk away from. This will change as our intimacy with God is established, for it is this that will build strong foundations out of a true understanding of who we really are and our own sense of value.

Throughout the gospel of John we read the statements that Jesus made about Himself. He was not afraid to do this because His sense of esteem and value were correctly founded and He was totally secure in who He was. To many they may seem strong, even arrogant statements, yet those who followed Him understood their meaning.

These statements were all based on two words: **'I am.'**

These words reveal His absolute, timeless existence – that He is from eternity to eternity, yet has stepped into time for a purpose, and that purpose concerns us. He reveals the love, the acceptance, the sense of value and purpose that God has for us.

These examples show us the strength of Jesus' security in His identity:

- *'I am He' [the Messiah],* (John 4:26).
- *'I tell you the truth, before Abraham was born, **I am**'* (John 8:58).
- *'I am the door'* (John 10: 9).
- *'I am the good shepherd'* (John 10:11, 14).
- *'I am the resurrection and the life'* (John 11:25).
- *'I am the way, the truth and the life'* (John 14:6).
- *'I am the true vine'* (John 15:1).

What does it mean?
Jesus is expressing confidently who He is. These are incredible statements. His intimacy with His Father gave Him a true understanding of His worth and value and He knew who He was. In the Old Testament these same words 'I am' have already been used to describe God.

When God spoke to Moses about leading the Israelites out of Egypt, Moses said to God, 'If I go to the Israelites and they ask me your name, then what shall I tell them?' The answer is so challenging and mysterious. God said to Moses, **'I AM WHO I AM.** Say to them: **"I AM** has sent you."' These are the same words that Jesus used in the above scriptures.

So what was Jesus doing? Surely expressing who He was in God in a very confident and secure manner. How can we apply this to our lives? It is a fact that we use the 'I am' words considerably and it is usually based on our reactions to what we think others have thought about us or even told us!

- 'I am no good'
- 'I am useless'
- 'I am not worth anything'
- 'I am rejected'
- 'I am a failure'
- 'I am finished'
- 'I am suicidal'

One day as Jesus was speaking to His disciples, He asked them a challenging and intriguing question, one which became crucial in their walk with Him. Matthew 16:13-17 explains it. Jesus asked them to tell Him who the people thought He was. They mentioned various people but then He turned the question back to them. 'Who do you say I am?' Peter had a great revelation, which Jesus rejoiced over. 'You are the Christ, the Son of the living God.' Once we know who **He** is then we can know who **we** are! And it is this that will give us the sense of value and worth we desire.

As we get to know Him then we can begin to change the way we think and talk. Our negative 'I am…' confessions can turn into positive ones that accurately describe our position in Christ.

Here are some positive statements we need to assimilate into our lives. There is nothing like learning by heart or rote to get something into you! Remember the way you were taught your maths tables at school? You went through them and through them and said them and said them until they were in you and part of you. So years later when someone asks you, 'What's seven times six?' you immediately know the answer – forty-two! Why? Because it's ingrained within you and it never goes away! As you continuously confess the positive 'I am's' they will get into you, into your heart and will become part of you. Make some choices and get on with it!

- *'I am a new creation"* (2 Corinthians 5:17). This is new life in Jesus. His life!
- *'I am accepted in Christ"* (Ephesians 1:6). This is totally unconditional!
- *'I am reconciled to God'* (2 Corinthians 5:18). No hostility or judgement from God but joined and united through Jesus.
- *'I am now a child of God'* (1 John 3:2). This means security and love in His family.
- *'I am free from **all** condemnation'* (Romans 8:1). There is no place for guilt, condemnation or accusation because I have a relationship with Jesus.
- *'I am loved with an everlasting love'* (Jeremiah 31:13). Nothing we can do can stop God loving us.
- *'I am chosen to be **in** Christ'* (Ephesians 1:4; 2:6; 2:10). We are, by grace, through faith, **in** Christ continually!

Jesus has made it possible through His life, death and

resurrection for us to receive His life, knowing that we can enter into all that He is. His prayer was that we might be one with Him and the Father. *'I in them and you in me'* (John 17:23). We are, as we believe.

How do we really see ourselves? Is it as a failure, rejected, with no sense of value or esteem? Let's begin to understand and accept how God sees us. Let's start where **He** starts. Let's look at ourselves from His perspective, because our beginning, end, and everything in between, is in Him.

The Psalmist wrote, *'I am like an olive tree flourishing in the house of God; I trust in Gods unfailing love for ever and ever.'* This is what to aim for in the way that we think. Please don't struggle to get there. Just accept the fact that God has accomplished it in His Son.

We can change our mindsets to a more positive pattern by choice and in conjunction with the power of the Holy Spirit working in us. Why don't you begin? It's up to you.

Consider the following. Because of Christ's redemption:
- I am a new creation of infinite worth.
- I am deeply loved.
- I am completely forgiven.
- I am fully pleasing.
- I am totally acceptable to God.
- I am absolutely complete in Christ!
- There has never been another person like me in the history of mankind. Nor will there ever be.
- God has made me an original, one of a kind, a special person.

Maybe it is this that we should confess rather than the negatives that we hear so often. Why don't you start?

6

Abba –
God as Father

Prophecy is one of the ways in which God communicates to the world and His people. Much of Scripture relates to this and prophecy has always been greatly significant to the society for which it was written. Prophecy has the ability to span generations and affect the future as well as time for which it was written.

The last prophecy in the last book of the Old Testament has this kind of relevance. Malachi 4:5-6 declares, *'See, I will send you the prophet Elijah before that great and dreadful day of the Lord comes. He will turn the hearts of the fathers to their children, and the hearts of the children to their fathers; or else I will come and strike the land with a curse.'*

In addition to the fact that the prophet Elijah is heralding the day of the Lord, another reason he is being sent is to do to with family relationships. Whether 'Elijah' in this context means a literal individual or a corporate expression in this context is debatable, but the fact that there will be an emphasis on fathers and children is undisputed.

This is significant to us because of the family problems that are rife in today's society. There is a clear lack of a father's love in so many families. Single parenting and divorce are on the increase and for whatever reason these things happen, they leave a gap where the love of a father to his children and children to their father should be. It also affects the way in which Christians perceive God as their Father and so often it is this very thing that hinders deep relationship and leaves Christians feeling insecure and worthless.

A considerable amount of the destructive power unleashed in this last century can be attributed to the world wars. Many families were, and still are, deeply affected when fathers were suddenly absent – often for years at a time. We are now in the fourth and fifth generations since 1914 where so many relationships with fathers were undermined. As we travel about ministering to people we meet many 'orphans'. They have parents, but the lack of love usually communicated through affection, with touches, kisses, cuddles and affirmation, has apparently left them with a deep sense of loss, almost bereavement. All this has brought conflict into our relationship with God and has brought about a wrong perception of God as a father.

Adoption
If we take a look at the meaning of 'adoption' in Scripture, we will begin to understand that God wants to show us how much He loves, accepts and values us!

Adoption was a familiar social event in Rome, and its ceremonies occupied a large and important place in its law. Through adoption a total stranger could become a member of the family. Such a person took on the family name, engaged in its sacrificial rites, and became a member of the house of his adoption.

The adopted one became, in the eyes of the law, a new creature, a new person. He was by the law's definition, '**born again into a new family.**'

Romans 8:14-16 tells us, '*Those who are led by the Spirit of God are sons of God. For you did not receive a spirit that makes you a slave again to fear, but you received the Spirit of sonship. And by him we cry, "Abba, Father." The Spirit himself testifies with our spirit that we are God's children.*'

Paul is teaching that God, revealing His grace through His son Jesus, brings us into a relationship with Himself, such that we become His 'sons'.

Adoption is the recognition and affirmation of our *sonship*. When we receive Jesus we become so united with the Father through Him that we receive the Spirit of sonship. We are able to know God as Jesus does.

When God sent His Son to redeem those that were under the law (Galatians 4:5-6), it became possible for us to receive adoption. For to those who are willing to receive Him, He sent the

Spirit of the eternal Son to testify in their hearts that they are sons of God, and to give them confidence to call God Father (Romans 8:15). This feeling of affection, love and confidence relates to children and sons, not to the servile spirit of slavery. Adoption is the process of taking and treating a stranger as one's own child. It is applied to Christians because God treats them as His children. He receives them into this relationship, though they were by nature strangers and enemies. When we are adopted into the family of God it gives us hope and the impetus to develop a relationship with God. Not only that, but we now have the privilege of calling Him a name that is so full of affection and intimacy...

'Abba'

This amazing word is mentioned only 3 times in Scripture and all of the references are in the New Testament (Galatians 4:6, Romans 8:15 and Mark 14:36). In each case it is used when calling on God in prayer.

In each of the 3 scriptures the term used is 'Abba Father' and the Greek word used with abba is *pater*. Together they mean 'dear Father' and the phrase reveals our true status as sons through adoption. This enables us to enter into the promise of 2 Corinthians 6:18, *'I will be a father to you and you will be my sons and daughters.'*

God said something similar to Solomon in 2 Samuel 7:13-14: *'He is the one who will build a house for my Name, and I will establish the throne of his kingdom for ever. I will be his father, and he will be my son.'*

In Aramaic the word is derived from baby language. *Abba* means daddy and *imma* means mummy. The word was widened to include older sons and daughters when addressing their father in terms of respect and honour.

So, *Abba* is the word spoken by infants and shows unquestioning trust. 'Father' expresses an intelligent apprehension of the relationship. 'Abba Father' – the two words together, expresss the love and intelligent confidence of a child. It is not unusual to repeat such terms of affection.

The right to call God 'Father' in a special and appropriate sense is open to all who have received the testimony of the Spirit, who cries 'abba'. It is our right because we are in Christ – in the family of God!

Slaves or servants were forbidden to address the head of a family using the word 'abba' because it was reserved for true children of the father.

There is no historical evidence in Jewish literature of 'abba' ever having been used to address God. So when Jesus used the term it was a radical and cultural break through. No Jew would ever have considered calling God 'abba'!

For Jesus, it clearly expressed His unique relationship with God – trust and obedience with an consistent response to His incomparable authority.

Amazingly we can call God by the same name that Jesus calls Him – 'Abba', daddy! This is the extent to which God values us, because He allows us to be intimate and affectionate with Him!

What the Holy Spirit says about Abba

Galatians 4:4-7 tells us, *'But when the time had fully come, God sent his Son, born of a woman, born under law, to redeem those under law, that we might receive the full rights of sons. Because you are sons, God sent the Spirit of his Son into our hearts, the Spirit who calls out, "Abba, Father." So you are no longer a slave, but a son and since you are a son, God has made you also an heir.'*

We've come out of living under the law that controlled us to **do** things. Now, through the grace of God, we have come into our full rights as sons. We had been slaves to the basic principles of this world with its fear, failure, anger, insecurity and persistent pressure to make us like slaves – always **doing** and never **being**.

Yet in the fulness of time God sent His son to redeem us so that He could adopt us, and we have received these rights as sons through the blood of Jesus.

> *'Yet to all who received him, to those who believed in his name, he gave the right to become children of God – children born not of natural descent, nor of human decision or a husband's will, but born of God.'* (John 1:12-13)

As we believe through repentance and faith we receive these rights because we receive the Spirit of the Son whom God has sent into our hearts. We have the Spirit because we are sons! We are sons because we have the Spirit.

Then the scripture says that the Spirit **calls** – communication begins. Where? Right in the core of our being, the heart. What is the Spirit calling? 'Abba Father'! Christianity begins with relationship with the Father. This is what family is about and he wants to draw us to Himself as soon as we are born again. Sonship changes us from being slaves into sons and heirs!

What we say about Abba

Romans 8:14-17 says, *'Those who are led by the Spirit of God are sons of God. For you did not receive a spirit that makes you a slave again to fear, but you received the Spirit of sonship. And by him we cry, "Abba, Father." The Spirit himself testifies with our spirit that we are God's children.'*

We all need to have an identity and a role. We are led by the Spirit who gives us an identity – the revelation of sonship and adoption as sons. We are no longer slaves to fear.

Look who is calling this time. It is not the Spirit within calling but it is we who do the calling! **We** are actually calling 'Abba, Father'! The Spirit gives witness in our hearts, but we do the calling; the communication, the confessing.

There is a progression from Galatians 4:6 to Romans 8:15. Firstly, it is the Spirit of God calling 'Abba, Father' but that naturally develops into us saying the same! So that which is in our hearts is now spoken out of our mouths. The first scripture relates to us believing in our hearts, but after that it is necessary to confess with our mouths. This then forms the basis for a closer relationship with our Father God. Every one of us has the Spirit of God calling 'abba' within, but not so many speak out of their mouth what is in their heart.

> *'"The word is near you; it is in your mouth and in your heart," that is, the word of faith we are proclaiming: That if you confess with your mouth, "Jesus is Lord," and believe in your heart that God raised him from the dead, you will be*

saved. For it is with your heart that you believe and are justified, and it is with your mouth that you confess and are saved.' (Romans 10:8-10)

Matthew 12:34 states, *'For out of the overflow of the heart the mouth speaks.'* So many people believe that they have no worth or value. It is not difficult to confess that when it is in your heart. But now that we know the Spirit of God has already begun calling 'Abba Father' within us, we can begin to say with our mouths what the Spirit is already saying in our heart! This becomes us confessing 'abba', which gives us the ability to enter into this new level of relationship with God.

> *'"Have faith in God," Jesus answered. "I tell you the truth, if anyone says to this mountain, 'Go, throw yourself into the sea,' and does not doubt in his heart but believes that what he says will happen, it will be done for him. Therefore I tell you, whatever you ask for in prayer, believe that you have received it, and it will be yours."'* (Mark 11:22-24)

God wants us to realise that through Him, we can deal with the mountains of doubt over our value and esteem! You confess with your mouth because you believe in your heart! We can take these scriptures and speak them out in the name of Jesus and stand against the doubts and fears that come in. Why? Because we have the Spirit of God within us introducing us to Abba Father!

What Jesus says about Abba
In Mark 14:32-36 we read, *'They went to a place called Gethsemane, and Jesus said to his disciples, "Sit here while I pray." He took Peter, James and John along with him, and he began to be deeply distressed and troubled. "My soul is overwhelmed with sorrow to the point of death," he said to them. "Stay here and keep watch." Going a little farther, he fell to the ground and prayed that if possible the hour might pass from him. "Abba, Father," he said, "everything is possible for you. Take this cup from me. Yet not what I will, but what you will."'*

This is the first reference where 'Abba' is mentioned and it is a very practical out-working of Jesus' relationship with His Father at the most difficult time of His life. Jesus is in the Garden of Gethsemane, just before He will go to the cross, where the most incredible conflict will take place. Jesus manifests deep anguish because of the impossible decision that He has to make. It is an amazing conflict of humanity and divinity.

In cold blood, it seems, He makes a difficult decision. It is the ultimate moment of choice and Jesus makes the right one. He says to the Father, '...not my will but yours be done.' His will becomes aligned with the Father's.

Jesus' response must also have been an emotional one, for in the midst of tremendous pressure, He cried out to His Father. It was the cry of intimacy, of unreasoning trust, a childlike response, a deep-seated cry from the heart to 'Abba Father'. The cry to God that no other Jew had ever made and only the Son of the Father **could** make.

This powerful response gives us hope for in the midst of our pain we can follow our Saviour and Lord and choose to align our wills with His and use the words 'Abba Father'. Words of trust, words that show us that even in our own hurt, doubts and fear we have a Father who will not only listen but cares enough to do something about things. The Father knew the Son had to go to the cross because that was the only way that His love for us could be shown and fulfilled. We can trust our God because He values us enough to give us the right to call Him 'Abba Father'.

The challenge to respond to Abba

> *'On the last and greatest day of the Feast, Jesus stood and said in a loud voice, "If anyone is thirsty, let him come to me and drink. Whoever believes in me, as the Scripture has said, streams of living water will flow from within him." By this he meant the Spirit, whom those who believed in him were later to receive. Up to that time the Spirit had not been given, since Jesus had not yet been glorified.'* (John 7:37-39)

Often there are blockages, doubts and fears in our response to

God. He trusts us and wants us to trust Him and respond to Him. There is a way that we can respond to God and that is to open ourselves to Jesus, as He calls us to do.

It was last day, that great day of the feast, that is the eighth day of the feast of Tabernacles as outlined in Leviticus 23:39. It was a Sabbath, the last feast day of the year, and distinguished by very remarkable ceremonies. It was a time of great joy, which broke out in loud shouting, particularly at the solemn moment when the priest, brought forth, in golden vessels, water from the stream of Siloam, which flowed under the temple-mountain, and poured it upon the altar. The words of Isaiah 12:3 were sung: *'With joy you will draw water from of the wells of Salvation.'*

It was at this time that Jesus, probably from some elevated position in the Temple, cried out, as if making a proclamation, saying that, 'If you really are thirsty come to me and drink because the water being poured out on the altar will not satisfy you!' He was talking about living water that would quench the deepest longings of the human spirit. Jesus was saying that if we believe in Him, if we drink from Him, out of our innermost being rivers of living water will flow.

It was as though He was comparing Himself with the river that flowed out from Ezekiel's Temple, which brought life everywhere it flowed. We need to come and drink of Him for within us are the words that the Holy Spirit has been consistently crying, 'Abba Father'. Surely as we drink of Him it is the revelation of 'Abba' that will flow forth from us in life giving power.

For such the Father seeks!

'Yet a time is coming and has now come when the true worshippers will worship the Father in spirit and truth, for they are the kind of worshippers the Father seek. God is spirit, and his worshippers must worship in spirit and in truth.' (John 4:23-24)

Worship is drinking of Him and as we drink the Father seeks us as we worship in spirit and truth. Let us worship from our spirits with reality for as we do the scripture says, 'that these are the kind of worshippers the Father seeks.' This is the revelation of 'Abba Father', our loving, affectionate and caring God who values us so much!

7

Sons or Slaves?

'There is nothing we can do to make God love us less.
There is nothing we can do to make God love us more.'

Why is it that there seems to be such a difference in the way each of us responds to God? We have seen clearly that we are 'sons of God' and this revelation has touched many of our lives dramatically. It has affected the way we live as Christians and the way we relate to the world and to our God as Father.

Some people find it very difficult to understand this foundational concept. It is crucial because it does affect how we see ourselves and how we think God sees us – perhaps more like a slave than a son!

We have seen in the previous chapters what God thinks about us, how He responds to us and how that gives us value and worth. However there is something else that is important to look at, which can affect each of us. In the first chapter, the younger son wanted to come home and was prepared to be a slave to gain the acceptance he was looking for. How can a son be a slave? It is not possible yet he made a decision to be one if it was required of him. The glorious thing is that he was received by his father as a son. He was restored in his sonship by receiving the ring, a seal of sonship, shoes (only sons wore shoes) and a cloak (which denoted a covering of righteousness – of being right with his father). Then a party ensued with the sacrifice of a fatted calf – the best. What grace from the father! Yet again he gave unconditionally and unreservedly.

It should have been a wonderful end to the story, but regretfully it doesn't finish with the redeemed son, because he had an older brother. This brother never left his home and yet his attitude was just as bad if not worse than that of his younger brother. ·

Luke 15:28-31 says, *'The older brother became angry and refused to go in. So his father went out and pleaded with him. But he answered his father, "Look! All these years I've been slaving for you and never disobeyed your orders. Yet you never gave me even a young goat so I could celebrate with my friends. But when this son of yours who has squandered your property with prostitutes comes home, you kill the fattened calf for him!" "My son," the father said, "you are always with me, and everything I have is yours."'*

When the older brother heard that his young brother had come home, we find that instead of rejoicing with everyone, he became very angry and refused to come into the house. It is amazing to see the kind of negative emotion that poured out as his father tried to reason with him. It is as though something deep inside him exploded.

A key to his hardhearted attitude was in the statement he made to his father, 'Look! All these years I've been slaving for you and never disobeyed your orders. Yet you never gave me even a young goat so I could celebrate with my friends.'

What is highlighted is the slavery of the elder brother; 'I've been slaving for you.' Here is a son who considered himself a slave, who in his own eyes had never broken the rules, had done everything right. Yet something was dreadfully wrong. He lived with the father, worked with the father, was with the father all of the time yet he never had the father's heart! He lived so close to the father, yet missed what was rightfully his! The father would have none of it and rightfully rebuked him, commenting appropriately, 'You are always with me and everything I have is yours!' But what the elder son did was to harden his heart.

Sons are sons! Born sons, always sons! They don't change into slaves when they feel like it. They are flesh and blood sons and cannot be anything else. So why is it that the elder brother thought he was a slave? His bitterness came out in his anger and he was harsh and legalistic just like the Pharisees who Jesus was referring to in the story. The elder brother judges his younger brother, who we actually see take responsibility for his wrongdoing. He also tries, without success, to control his father in the situation.

This is a picture of many Christians who have a wrong perception of who they are. How can we be slaves if we are in Christ? We are sons! We are not slaves, yet so many of us think otherwise and act accordingly. But we are who we are – sons of God! Born into sonship by the Spirit of God through the death and resurrection of the Son of God. So why do we act as slaves? Even as the father was with the elder brother, our heavenly Father is with us. As the father said that the elder brother had everything, is it not true that we have the same from our heavenly Father through Jesus?

The fact is that the elder brother did not act as a slave would. A slave would never have responded, or reacted, or have the same attitude as he did!

A slave is someone controlled by a dominating authority. It is someone who is the legal property of another, is bound to absolute obedience and is often a helpless victim worn down by work. It is someone who is often born into slavery and is under a legal bondage to serve, whatever the consequence. Slavery is depersonalising, devaluing. There is no worth, no value, no acceptance, no affirmation, no nothing! When you think of slavery, you think of the Children of Israel under the bondage of the Egyptians!

The father of the two sons was in fact the very opposite of anything like this. He was a man of such grace and mercy; one who had compassion and who loved his sons unconditionally and unreservedly. He was no slave owner or taskmaster!

When the Law of Moses was established in the Old Testament, there came with it regulations, rules and requirements. Demands and expectations were not far behind and there were groups of leaders who became obsessed with duty and external conduct. This led to harsh and judgemental pronouncements being an integral part of the religious system of the day. There was no room for the joyful obedience of a heart response, only a gritted, grim determination to obey.

Wasn't the older brother just like that? Somehow he had grasped this rather than a sense of grace and unconditional love. The problem is that this would never give him value and worth only resentment and bitterness as he tried out of a sense of duty to be what he thought others wanted him to be. Jesus shows us the way to something else. He brings with Him a revolution of the heart, which can set captives free from a system, that brings only guilt and condemnation, and leads to the devaluation of self-worth and self-esteem. Jesus speaks about a freedom that only sons can enjoy, and **we are sons!**

> 'To the Jews who had believed him, Jesus said, "If you hold to my teaching, you are really my disciples. Then you will know the truth, and the truth will set you free." They answered him; "We are Abraham's descendants and have never been slaves of anyone. How can you say that we shall be set free?" Jesus replied, "I tell you the truth, everyone who sins is a slave to sin. Now a slave has no permanent place in the family, but a son belongs to it forever. So if the Son sets you free, you will be free indeed."'   (John 8:31-36)

Isn't this the way forward for the older brother and us? The father said, 'You are always with me.' As a son he was and as sons in Christ so are we!

Grace

> 'For the law was given through Moses; grace and truth came through Jesus Christ.'   (John 1:17)

We have received the grace of God. Grace is a favour that is given without expectation of return. It is the absolute freedom of the loving-kindness of God to humanity. The only motive is open-heartedness and a sense of wanting to give without any return. It is unearned and unmerited favour. To show grace is to extend favour or kindness to one that doesn't deserve it, and can never earn it. As we receive God's acceptance by grace our sense of value will increase. If we try to earn this grace by our own works, we will feel devalued because we can do nothing to attain to the level God demands.

We do not deserve grace; it is favour extended out of the heart of the giver. Grace is absolutely and totally free. God will never demand that we pay Him back. We couldn't anyway! Grace is unconditional with no strings attached, so we can claim this grace as our very own, by faith.

Ephesians 1:6-8 states,

> *'To the praise of his glorious grace, which he has freely given us in the One he loves. In him we have redemption through his blood, the forgiveness of sins, in accordance with the riches of God's grace that he lavished on us with all wisdom and understanding.'*

> *'For it is by grace you have been saved, through faith – and this not from yourselves, it is the gift of God – not by works, so that no one can boast.'* (Ephesians 2:8-9)

Surely we would take the credit if we could! But we can't if it is a gift. We cannot earn it!

2 Corinthians 12:9 tells us, *'"My grace is sufficient for you, for my power is made perfect in weakness." Therefore I will boast all the more gladly about my weaknesses, so that Christ's power may rest on me.'*

Learning that His grace is sufficient in every situation is not easy, but because it is **His grace** it is possible. When we try it is impossible!

Someone has said, 'Christianity is both the hardest and the easiest religion in the world. The easiest because we come with nothing, with empty hands to the foot of the Cross. And yet it is the hardest for that very same reason, because our pride and selfishness does not want us to accept that we should come with open hands. We feel that we must need to bring something; we want to contribute to our own salvation, to be the one who says we are in control rather than God.'

The pressure to do!
Do better!
Try harder!
Love deeper!
Give more!

This is the pressure that so many are under. If the gospel, which is God's love to us, is only a challenge to do better, we are in trouble because we won't get to where God wants us to fully enter into His purposes.

So often we have tried to do better and failed. Whether we try to keep more rules or carry out more activities, it only results in discouragement and disillusionment.

Grace says, 'This is what I want to do for you. You don't have to anything.' It is unconditional, a free gift. We are His children and He loves us! Learning to rest in this promise is where we start.

The three temptations of Jesus that we saw earlier were intended to lure Him into proving Himself, to prove His identity and calling. Yet Jesus had no need to prove anything. If God gives you identity that's enough! I don't want to prove anything, just experience God's love because my worth is not dependent on how well I perform.

Performance mentality

If we succeed then we expect God to be pleased. However, if we continue with this mindset, then when we inevitably fail we will be left angry, disappointed and disillusioned. We will then judge ourselves and fall into the failure syndrome of critically judging others in the same way.

Cain was a prime example of this:

> *'In the course of time Cain brought some of the fruits of the soil as an offering to the Lord. But Abel brought fat portions from some of the firstborn of his flock. The Lord looked with favour on Abel and his offering, but on Cain and his offering he did not look with favour. So Cain was very angry, and his face was downcast. Then the Lord said to Cain, "Why are you angry? Why is your face downcast? If you do what is right, will you not be accepted? But if you do not do what is right, sin is crouching at your door; it desires to have you, but you must master it." Now Cain said to his brother Abel, "Let's go out to the field." And while they were in the field, Cain attacked his brother Abel and killed him.'*

(Genesis 4:3-8)

It is so amazing that, in this case, murder was not so far away from an anger that was chiefly directed at God.

The revelation of God's rest

Someone has said that we are meant to be human 'beings' not human 'doings'!

The law says, 'I ought to and I must do it on my own to prove that I can.'

Grace says, 'I want to and I can do it in Him for He lives through me.'

Focusing on rules will never lead to obedience. Focusing on Him will release the grace to get through. The legalistic attitude of the elder brother indicates a restlessness, which would have affected every part of his life.

However, there is a place of rest in our relationship with God and it is here that we shall not want! Psalm 23:1-3 (NKJV) says, *'The Lord is my shepherd; I shall not want. He makes me to lie down in green pastures; he leads me beside the still waters* (or waters of rest). *He restores my soul.'* The call of God is rest!

Again in Hebrews 4:9-12 we read, *'There remains, then, a Sabbath-rest for the people of God; for anyone who enters God's rest also rests from his own work, just as God did from his. Let us, therefore, make every effort to enter that rest, so that no one will fall by following their example of disobedience. For the word of God is living and active. Sharper than any double-edged sword, it penetrates even to dividing soul and spirit, joints and marrow; it judges the thoughts and attitudes of the heart.'*

After God made the heavens and the earth, He rested on the seventh day. He created man and woman on the sixth day so they began their life in God's rest! **Do we?** God's rest is a place where there is no performance, control, striving, restlessness or perfectionism. In God's grace we can truly rest in Him!

> *'Come to me, all of you who are tired from carrying heavy loads, and I will give you rest. Take my yoke and put it on you, and learn from me, because I am gentle and humble in spirit; and you will find rest. For the yoke I will give you is easy, and the load I will put on you is light.'* (Matthew 11:28-30)

If we give up trying and just come to Him as sons, we will know the reality of rest in Him. The Lord's yoke is easy because He takes the weight. **Let go and let God!**

8

'Does She Take Sugar?'

A TV programme sometime ago drew attention to the frustrations of the physically disabled that are presumed to have some mental malfunction because they use a wheelchair. People with a speech impairment, for example, have had their mental capacity totally misunderstood. Various film dramatisations have gone some way towards drawing this problem to our attention, and have highlighted the wonderful determination of disabled people striving to receive acceptance and respect.

Function and identity

As we grow up, we learn to associate identity with ability. Quite simply, if we have a burst water pipe, we call a plumber. We look in the telephone book under the 'plumbing' section and from the list of names choose 'John Smith – Plumber.' Knowing that he has identified himself in this way, we trust that he has the skill to mend our pipe. Because John Smith can function as a plumber, he has identity, value and worth. If a physical or mental disability makes it difficult to have an identity in this way, it can seem impossible to feel any sense of worth or value.

Disability in any form, whether it be physical, mental or emotional strips away all the reasons to be accepted. Until recently, there has been little or no education in the understanding of disability. Having lived with Multiple Sclerosis for 27 years, I have witnessed a whole spectrum of experience. 'Where would Chris like to sit?' is a well used question. My interjection could be, 'Can't you show me enough dignity and respect to ask **me**?' I have also, not a few times, found myself somewhere I didn't intend to be, because at a conference or a meeting someone decides I would like to be in another part of the room and takes me there without asking, or even more to the point, without me suggesting it! All of this behaviour, with the kindest of intentions can reinforce feelings of lack of self-worth, confidence, identity and value.

The summer of 1971 was to be the most memorable in our lives. Joanna, our first baby was ten months old, we had our first home and I was enjoying life. I wanted to take Joanna to the swimming pool but I had been feeling some soreness in my hands so I called in at the doctor to check there was nothing to stop me going swimming. To my surprise, I found myself having a very thorough examination. Steve was called home from the office and I saw a consultant immediately. It all seems very dramatic now, but I am grateful for the speed at which my doctor worked because, after being sent to hospital that day for tests, I woke up the next morning having lost the strength and feeling in all of my left side. I could only walk slowly, dragging my leg and I didn't have enough strength in my left hand to lift a teaspoon to stir my tea!

That day, as I sat in a side room at the hospital, waiting to be taken to the chapel for the Sunday service, I experienced the most traumatic challenge to my identity and self-image. Until then, my role as a wife and mother had been all I wanted. I had been a legal secretary until just before the baby was born, which I really enjoyed, but I loved being a mum. Now I was sitting in a side ward, unable to walk, with a group of people I couldn't relate to. There were wheelchairs, walking frames, tall metal things with what looked like plastic bags of blood connected to people's arms, and it seemed as if everyone was very old or dying. Fear and confusion overwhelmed me! Would I ever walk again? Would I be able to hold my baby? What about Steve – how would he cope? So many questions flooded my mind.

I returned home after a few days and was treated there for the next few weeks, but life never returned to normal, as can be the case after a traumatic experience. Although physically I went into remission for two or three years, something had changed in me. I could no longer rely on the safe identity structure which I had created. I chose to wilfully deny the fears, yet deep within me I knew that nothing was certain any more. All I could do was ask

God that I would be able to be all that my children needed through their nurturing years. He answered this prayer but not in the way I expected! As I became less and less able to do things for my girls, it became more and more obvious that our communication of love was all that mattered.

I have seen through my family a very clear picture of the love of Father God. You see my family don't love me and value me because I am disabled. Nor do they love me despite the fact that I am disabled. They love me unconditionally! We talk, we laugh, we cry together. They hate MS and all it means, but it has nothing to do with their feelings for me. Why? Its because they value me for who I am and not what I do!

For several years after my initial attack of MS it was possible to live in a measure of unreality. I was healthy enough to pretend that everything was normal. I couldn't face the truth that nothing was certain any more and that at any time I could relapse. I couldn't even say the word Multiple Sclerosis and certainly found it almost impossible to talk about it.

As I increasingly found it difficult to hide my physical decline, I felt more and more embarrassed by the way I was. How could Steve preach about God's healing power when I was not healed? One day as I sat, feeling helpless and hopeless the reality of this scripture deeply affected me.

John 8:32 says, *'You will know the truth and the truth will set you free'* or in other words 'you will face reality and you will be set free in the problem'!

So I chose to face the fact that I had MS and not to be ashamed or embarrassed about it. As I made that choice, the truth has given me the ability to be emotionally and spiritually free, although I am not free in body.

The day I went into hospital all those years ago, God gave the same promise independently to Steve and my mother – 'fear not for she shall be made whole.' I am still waiting to be free **from** MS but I do feel amazingly free **in** it!

Disability, whether physical or mental, creates a feeling of immediate disadvantage in every social encounter. Sitting in a wheelchair, you have to look up to every one! No wonder it's easy to feel inferior, inadequate and worthless! It's like having a notice around your neck, which says to anyone who looks at you 'This is the area in my life, which causes the deepest pain.' It's neither acceptable nor appropriate to communicate at a private or personal level with everyone we meet. Most of us choose very carefully whom we invite into the deep hidden areas of our minds and emotions, yet it seems that to be disabled means a forfeiting of that right. When I go to the shops in my power wheelchair, people look at me, smile, say hello, and help me if I need it. But would they be so friendly if I didn't have my wheelchair? When they smile, look or speak, is it me or is it the wheelchair they notice? You see all of these people pass by and I know nothing about them except the kind word or helpful gesture, yet they see me in all my vulnerability. It's a challenge to retain a sense of self-worth while asking a total stranger to reach a tin of soup for me from the supermarket shelf!

Disabled people have become a sub-culture with similar prejudices and disadvantages to those endured by other social, racial and religious minorities. Societies and clubs have been created so that people with similar problems can meet, and these have been so valuable and a lifeline to many people. But we have also noticed, having visited these places, a sense of resigned separateness from normality. It is very easy for a disabled person to be conditioned by the insensitive inappropriate behaviour of healthy people to expect to be patronised, disrespected or even ignored.

Some people who are able-bodied and healthy have a strange perception of disabled people. This has been evident in the way they talk either to or about them. I remember being ignored by someone who knew me very well the first time they saw me in a wheelchair. They talked the whole time to my companion, not looking at me once. I'm sure this is due to embarrassment and fear.

The human reaction to something outside of our perspective of what is 'normal' is to recoil and feel distinctly uncomfortable. A person who is disabled often experiences this reaction in every-day life. No wonder it is easier to stay in the security of the home or day centre.

It's very difficult for a person with an obvious disability to know what to do in a meeting where there is a ministry time. Is it right to always go for prayer? If you do, it's possible to feel at everyone's mercy, such as the people with apparent faith for a miracle, or those who discern that there must be sin in my life or generational demons. I have been very open to the possibility of all these things, but when you become vulnerable and yet these things happen, it is difficult not to feel disappointed and reluctant to be put in that position again. Of course, if I don't go for prayer I could be missing my healing. What a conflict!

It would appear that the rules in prayer ministry are often changed when there are people with disabilities in the congregation. I have had hands laid on me unexpectedly in the middle of a meeting by people I didn't know. This, even with the kindest and most compassionate intentions, really doesn't encourage a feeling of self-respect or worth, because the decision whether or not to be prayed for is taken out of my hands.

God has promised that He will heal me and despite all I have said I am grateful for all the prayers I have received. I just want you to know some of the difficulties people like me face so that barriers can be broken down and mutual respect, understanding and love established.

A person with a disability is often thought of in the following ways, all of which are demeaning and devaluing:

1. Automatically has a mental disability, so talk slowly and loudly.
2. Very sensitive, angry and easily hurt, so overprotect, be careful what you say.
3. Cannot take responsibility for life, so don't expect anything from her or him.
4. Cannot make good choices, so don't give him or her any.
5. Does not have a sexual need, so don't worry about that!
6. Is unable to work and wouldn't really want to.
7. Should only associate with other disabled people because 'It's nice for them.'
8. Is disabled for a 'spiritual reason'. She or he needs a lot of ministry.
9. Is an embarrassment? What should we do with them? Be friendly – if we see them!

It's wonderful to know that however we look on the outside, our value is in the constant unchanging love and acceptance of our heavenly Father. I really believe it gives Him such great joy when we recognise and learn how to apply these great truths in our lives by making right choices in attitude and behaviour. But these things don't make Him love us more, or accept us more, or value us more.

I realise now that God values me, like you as a person, not because I have a disability, not despite my disability, but simply because Scripture says He delights in me and I believe it!

9

The Process of Healing –
What do we do When it Hurts?

A lifetime of low self worth and value usually means that there is a huge amount of emotional pain deep inside. Father God wants to come with His love and heal the wounds of the past.

If a friend says to you, 'You look very nice today,' how do you respond? A lack of worth and value replies, 'don't be silly' or 'you're joking,' or you think they don't mean it because you know it's not true! Confidence in your godly identity replies 'thank you' and creates a feeling of wellbeing.

Steps to Healing
1. **Recognition.** Admit how you feel.
2. **Repentance.** Say sorry to God for holding on to the pain, sometimes unintentionally.
3. **Forgiveness.** Let go of any judgement in your heart to:
    i.   Yourself – for 'getting into this mess.'
    ii. Others – people who have hurt you.
    iii. God – ask forgiveness for blaming Him for the way you are and your situation.
4. **Open yourself to the presence of the Holy Spirit.** This is an act of the will and also of faith.
5. **Release the pain, and anger.** Take it to the cross.

'Surely he took up our infirmities and carried our sorrows.'
(Isaiah 53:4)

'For we do not have a high priest who is unable to sympathise with our weaknesses, but we have one who has been tempted in every way, just as we are – yet was without sin.' (Hebrews 4:15)

It is so important that we see that Jesus has identified fully and completely with us. When we see that, it gives us confidence to trust and let go.

> *'You number my wanderings; put my tears into your bottle; are they not in your book? When I cry out to you, then my enemies will turn back; this I know, because God is for me. In God I have put my trust; I will not be afraid. What can man do to me?'*   (Psalm 56:8-11 NKJV)

'Tear bottles' were common at that time and were often buried with the person who had died. The Father is saying that He has His own 'bottle' for us, to collect our tears and bury them never to be seen again! As we let go He will keep His word and begin healing.

> *'They went to a place called Gethsemane, and Jesus said to his disciples, "Sit here while I pray." He took Peter, James and John along with him, and he began to be deeply distressed and troubled. "My soul is overwhelmed with sorrow to the point of death," he said to them. "Stay here and keep watch." Going a little farther, he fell to the ground and prayed that if possible the hour might pass from him. "Abba, Father," he said, "everything is possible for you. Take this cup from me. Yet not what I will, but what you will."'*   (Mark 14:32-36)

Even Jesus came to a place of decision and as He chose to submit to His father's will, He called to 'Abba Father' and victory came. We can do the same! It is crucial to always remember that although Abba Father wants to reveal Himself, it is conditional upon an act of will on our part.

6. **Receive the love of the Father.** By faith we receive the love of the Father which cleanses us from the effects of the past and heals our wounds.

From your new place of wholeness, with an understanding of who you are – a child of God, accepted, valued and loved – these points are summarised for you as a reminder as you work out your salvation.

> *'Therefore, my dear friends, as you have always obeyed –*
> *not only in my presence, but now much more in my absence –*
> *continue to work out your salvation with fear and trembling,*
> *for it is God who works in you to will and to act according to*
> *his good purpose.'* (Philippians 2:12-13)

- You can defend your own belief systems in the face of strong opinions.
- You can absorb the love of God which brings you adequacy.
- Remember who you are (your 'identity').
- Have a non-defensive attitude. Take care how you protect your image or feelings.
- You needn't feel any guilt if others disapprove.
- You needn't worry about yesterday or tomorrow.
- You can have the confidence to deal with problems.
- Be open and understanding with people.
- You are equal and have equal standing with others – neither superior nor inferior!
- You can accept praise from others and believe it.
- You can apply God's love and acceptance to others.
- You can be sensitive to others and their own needs.
- Recognise that you have value and worth to others, to yourself and to God.

> *'And God is able to make all grace abound to you, so that in*
> *all things at all times, having all that you need, you will*
> *abound in every good work.'* (2 Corinthians 9:8)

10

Risky Living –
The Real Walk of Faith!

Life is a risk or a walk of faith. There isn't much difference in spiritual terms. So as you go on in God beyond your healing be determined to live in victory.

Understanding and living with a positive self-image
It's not easy to change a belief system that has been in place for many years, maybe even a lifetime. We need to change from confessing we are a nobody, to know and understand the person we were created to be.

These 3 statements form the foundation of a positive self-image.
● I belong
● I am worth something
● I can do it!

Belonging gives a sense and awareness of being wanted, accepted and cared for. Value comes from acceptance. As we feel accepted, we can feel secure in who we are and will be more and more able to value our own ideals and opinions. This will lead to a feeling of adequacy, which, when built on present as well as past achievements, will provide an ability to cope with life.

By understanding the place of faith and making right choices, it is possible to develop a healthy self-image. The following will help:

1. Develop a healthy and personal relationship with Jesus
Our 2½-year-old granddaughter loves to talk! She jumps onto our laps and says; 'Shall we talk?' We love those moments and listening to her chatter is so precious. How much more does

'Abba' value those times when we talk with Him? This kind of communication will lead into a deep sense of communion where prayer, intercession and worship will flow.

With the realisation that He responds unconditionally to us even in our imperfections, we can learn to forgive the faults and imperfections in others. Why? Because we are new creations!

2 Corinthians 5:17 says, *'Therefore, if anyone is in Christ, he is a new creation; the old has gone, the new has come!'*

As you open yourself to the unconditional love of God, you will be challenged by the One who is the Truth to believe the truth about yourself. This will mean removing the masks and facades that have been built up over the years and facing reality. Then there will be no need to find an identity in anyone but God.

2. Consider the life-giving power of the Scriptures

The Word of God is living, powerful and active. Hebrews 4:12, *'For the word of God is living and active. Sharper than any double-edged sword, it penetrates even to dividing soul and spirit, joints and marrow; it judges the thoughts and attitudes of the heart.'*

It is therefore important to understand the powerful nature of the Word of God. The uniqueness of Scripture leads to a personal, positive application of its truth and as we read it we can be washed, cleansed and rebuilt. There is a power to bring revelation that is in found in no other book.

Song of Solomon 1:2 even speaks of the kiss of God. *'Let him kiss me with the kisses of his mouth.'* It really is that personal! One interpretation would say that this is God kissing us in our spirits with His word – His *rhema* – the story, sentence, phrase or word that leaps off the page into our situation. This is God speaking to us! We live by God's Word. Matthew 4:4 says, *'Jesus answered, "It is written: 'Man does not live on bread alone, but on every word that comes from the mouth of God.'"'* Understanding these truths and practising them will build a new confidence and security in the word of God and into us.

3. Learn to be honest

Denial is part of your old ways and habits. Being honest with

God, yourself and then others is the way forward. Mercy, which is undeserved, is available by the grace of God.

> *'He who conceals his sins does not prosper, but whoever confesses and renounces them finds mercy.'* (Proverbs 28:13)

When we conceal we push down and bury our problem and the pain is stored up. Confession will bring release. Remember, we must never bury our problems alive!

4. Understand that mind-sets can be challenged and changed

Scripture shows us that we can have a 'renewed' mind. By taking responsibility and learning to take our thoughts captive, we can, by God's grace, have the mind of Christ – a sound mind. We can therefore learn to change the way we think from the negative, which brings low self-esteem, to the positive, which brings a sense of worth and value.

'For God hath not given us the spirit of fear; but of power, and of love, and of a sound mind' (2 Timothy 1:7 KJV). The gift of God is a sound mind and self-control.

'And the peace of God, which transcends all understanding, will guard your hearts and your minds in Christ Jesus. Finally, brothers, whatever is true, whatever is noble, whatever is right, whatever is pure, whatever is lovely, whatever is admirable – if anything is excellent or praiseworthy – think about such things' (Philippians 4:7-8). Do you see the way the mind is? Through the Holy Spirit we can guard it and by His power and our choice we can think on good things.

> *'Since, then, you have been raised with Christ, set your hearts on things above, where Christ is seated at the right hand of God. Set your minds on things above, not on earthly things. For you died, and your life is now hidden with Christ in God.'* (Colossians 3:1-3)

Because of our position hidden in Christ, we can not only set our hearts on things above but also our minds and the way we think!

'For though we live in the world, we do not wage war as the world does. The weapons we fight with are not the weapons of the world. On the contrary, they have divine power to demolish strongholds. We demolish arguments and every pretension that sets itself up against the knowledge of God, and we take captive every thought to make it obedient to Christ.' (2 Corinthians 10:3-5)

Do you see that our fight is a spiritual fight and not one that we can wage with the weapons of this world? Because we are in Christ, we have the ability to demolish all arguments and temptations that come to us and take them captive. When we sense a feeling of condemnation or self-rejection, we can deal with that accusation in the power of the Holy Spirit and make it captive, bringing it into obedience to Christ.

James 4:2 clearly says that 'we do not have because we do not ask!' Maybe it is time to take action and begin to renew our minds and break down some of these old habits and mind sets.

5. Understanding our 'self-talk'

Everyone talks to him or herself. A person with low self-esteem would usually perceive anything that happens to them in a negative way, taking the blame, being self-critical and feeling inferior. This kind of negativity can lead to depression and deep rejection.

The Bible tells us in James 1:19 that everyone should be quick to listen, slow to speak and slow to become angry. In every situation, listen, with understanding and a renewed mind, challenge your self-talk and respond accordingly.

6. The Power of communication

A new sense of self-worth and value will mean that your communication style may need adjusting, so we have listed some points for your consideration:

● Know peace; learn to rest day by day in the Holy Spirit.
● Give clear understanding to others as you consider their point of view and their feelings.
● Learn to prepare your communication; think before you

speak.
- Be decisive; be clear be concise.
- Don't be afraid to negotiate in a conversation and learn the difference between a right and a wrong compromise.
- Conversation is an art to be learned, so don't be afraid of 'small talk', learn to listen, don't interrupt, use humour when appropriate and learn to understand 'non-verbal' signs.
- It's important to use self-disclosure with sensitivity. Being vulnerable in a wrong context can cause problems and expose you to criticism, unhelpful counsel and a whole host of unwise comments.
- Learn to receive as well as give compliments.
- Don't be afraid of eye contact. Someone has said, "no one can make you feel inferior without your consent."

7. Be Assertive
In the society in which we live there have tended to be two types of recognised behaviour:

i. Aggressive
An aggressive person has a tendency toward being domineering, forceful, insensitive, hostile, hurtful, prejudiced, abusive of power and also threatened and isolated.

ii. Passive
A passive person has a tendency toward being compliant, subservient, resigned, indecisive, self-blaming and insignificant.

However there is a third type which is the way God created us to be.

iii. Assertive
An assertive person is confident in who they are and who they can be. They are positive, decisive, sincere, insistent, team-spirited, creative, accepted and acceptable, effective at communication and able to cope with criticism and be intimate.

Confidence in who we are in God means that we can say 'yes' or even 'no,' be successful, make mistakes, change our minds, make our own decisions, cope with any consequences, have an opinion, have feelings and emotions and appropriately show them!

And finally always remember as you take faltering steps towards change. You may fail, but you are **NEVER** a failure! God's grace will sustain you and His love will uphold you.

❖ ❖ ❖ ❖

If you have enjoyed this book and would like to help us to send a copy of it and many other titles to needy pastors in the **Third World**, please write for further information or send your gift to:

Sovereign World Trust, P.O. Box 777, Tonbridge, Kent TN11 0ZS, United Kingdom

or to the **'Sovereign World'** distributor in your country.